So... You Decided to Write a Book

The Ultimate Guide to Writing and Publishing Your Book

by
Douglas J Boggs

OLIVE PUBLISHING, LLC

Make sure to leave a review of our book online!

Find us at:

https://olivepublishingllc.com/

Copyright ©2023 by Olive Publishing, LLC. All rights reserved.

No part of this publication may be reproduced, stored in a retrieval system, or transmitted in any form or by any means, electronic, mechanical, photocopying, recording, scanning, or otherwise, without either the prior written permission of the publisher. For information address the Permissions Dept., Olive Publishing, LLC, 30 N Gould St., Suite 4000, Sheridan, WY, 82801.

Limit of Liability/Legal Disclaimer: While the publisher and author have used their best efforts in preparing this book, they make no legal representations and any information contained in this book is not intended to constitute legal or professional advice. This book is specifically designed to assist in helping writers create and publish their books. The advice and strategies contained herein may not be suitable for your situation. Neither the publisher nor author shall be liable for any loss of profit or any other commercial damages, including but not limited to special, incidental, consequential, or other damages.

Every reasonable attempt has been made to trace copyright holders of material reproduced in this book, but if any has been inadvertently overlooked, the publishers would be glad to hear from them.

Edited and formatted by Kat at Genesis Design and Editing, LLC.

Cover art concept/design – Nicole M. Eisenhauer

Library of Congress Cataloging-to-Publication Data:

Boggs, Douglas J – So, You've Decided to Write a Book - The Ultimate Guide to Writing and Publishing Your Book

Douglas j Boggs - "An Olive Publishing, LLC book" First U.S. Edition 2023

1. Publishing 2. writing 3. hybrid 4. self-publishing 5. traditional 6. editing 7. marketing 8. Title 9. Douglas J Boggs 10. Olive publishing, LLC

ISBN(s) – 978-1-7364715-8-6 eBook; 978-1-7364715-9-3 softcover

https://olivepublishingllc.com

10 7 8 3 6 9 5 4 2 1

Contents

- SO...YOU DECIDED TO WRITE A BOOK .... - 1 -
- CREATING YOUR OUTLINE FOR WRITING A BOOK .... - 7 -
- CREATING YOUR SCENES AND SETTINGS ....- 19 -
- FOLLOWING YOUR OUTLINE TO WRITE YOUR BOOK.............................. - 29 -
- A QUERY LETTER TO FIND YOUR AGENT .... - 63 -
- MARKETING YOUR BOOK... - 67 -
- CREATING A PODCAST .... - 77 -
- CREATING A FOLLOWING .... - 81 -
- BUILD YOUR ONLINE PRESENCE.. - 85 -
- MASS MEDIA PROMOTION .... - 89 -
- THE BUSINESS OF WRITING .... - 93 -
- BECOMING A THOUGHT LEADER AND BRAND .... - 97 -
- TRADEMARK YOUR BRAND .... - 103 -
- PROS AND CONS OF SELF, HYBRID AND TRADITIONAL PUBLISHING- 107 -
- JOIN THE OLIVE PUBLISHING FAMILY .... - 113 -

SO...YOU DECIDED TO WRITE A BOOK

There are more writers today than ever before in history. Technology has always been the driving force of the growth of writing. The written word began thousands of years ago in the area now known as Iraq when the Anunnaki created a language on tablets called Cuneiform. However, once it was written it still took thousands of years before the printing press was invented. No one truly knows when the first printing press was invented or who invented it, but the oldest known printed text originated in China during the first millennium A.D. with *The Diamond Sutra*, a Buddhist book from Dunhuang, China, dating from around 868 A.D. during the Tang Dynasty. This oldest known printed book was the start of a revolution. Since then, the distribution of thoughts through print have created governments, started, and ended wars, created poetry, songs, religion and so much more. The written word has helped shape the human species to what it is today and continues to mold its future. Modern technology has created an ever-widening variety of means for writers to find ways to express themselves in the varied platforms, markets, and distribution options available.

The mystery therein begs the question to most writers of "How do I even begin to write my book?" This can be a rather daunting task and holds quite a bit of mystery for most people. But Olive Publishing, LLC, wanted to help change all of that. I have authored numerous books and, together with Olive Publishing, have helped many other authors get their books completed and published.

When I began writing my first book, the critically acclaimed "Quantum of Justice", I realized early that it is imperative to create an outline for the book. Just like building a house, or creating a product to be manufactured, it all starts with a set of plans, drawings, or schematics as a foundation with which to build from. Everything that lasts has a solid foundation. The pyramids in Egypt were built with massive stones placed perfectly together to give it its solid foundation that has made them last for millennia.

When I first started writing, I didn't know how to create an outline for a book. In my situation, my book developed out of my court case against Wells Fargo

Bank. As the court case unfolded over the four years of litigation, it created the outline itself. I wasn't aware of the power of this until later. Since then, the other books that I have written or helped develop are based on outlines with which to give the plot and structure of the story a guidepost.

I come across so many writers that have begun creating their books with no outline and they tend to get lost along the way as they follow their creative tangents down roads that can lead them nowhere. It can be easy for a writer with no outline to get lost in their own story. The outline is there as a touchstone for each chapter to help the writer stay on track for their desired plot line. It helps the writer stay focused so they can guide the reader to exactly where they want them to go in the story.

Whether the book is fiction or non-fiction it is best to begin with an outline as a place to start. So, how do you create an outline that will work for you? Not all outlines are the same as not every writer thinks and works the same. But for you, the author who is saying where do I go next, I have developed an outline for an outline to not only write your book, but also to guide you through the process of creating and publishing your book so you can get it out into the world.

There are many writers that say they just want to "get it out there so people can read it and enjoy." That's fine, however, it is for this reason that most writers don't make much money. The trick is to more than want to get your book out there for people to read and enjoy, but you also want people to pay for the book so you can earn a profit from all your hard work. Some books come to writers easily and quickly, but many books can take a writer years of their lives to complete. Wouldn't you want to see a return for all of that effort?

Writing a book is one thing, but following that there is the process of editing, formatting, typesetting, artwork, production, and publication. Then comes the process of distributing the book. However, there will be no distribution of anything if you are unable to find the people who want to read your book! But don't be discouraged, you won't do this alone as the publication process is comprised of a team of people to help make your book successful.

In today's world of self-publishing, we have seen nearly anyone, and everyone, create a book. But even though it looks like anyone can write and publish a book, but only 10% of self-published books ever sell more than 100 copies. This is due primarily because the author may have the determination to write a book but does not know the proper steps following the writing. "Oh, you mean there is more I have to do?" Authors must understand that the writing is just the beginning stages of the life of their book. You then need to advertise, market, promote and get the word out for people to find your book.

I have outlined a business model for an author to use to not only create and write their book but to also help them through the maze of other tasks that are needed to get their book out into the world so it can be found, purchased, read, and reviewed for more and more people to find.

But before we get ahead of ourselves let's start at the beginning.

CREATING YOUR OUTLINE FOR WRITING A BOOK

Here are some basic steps to help you create an outline for authoring a book:

1. Begin by brainstorming your ideas. Start by jotting down all the ideas you have for your book. This could include a general concept, themes, characters, scenes, plot points, or anything else that comes to mind. As you do this practice, your outline will begin to create itself.

2. The next step is to organize your ideas. Once you have a list of ideas, you can organize them into categories or sections. For example, if you're writing a non-fiction book, you might categorize your ideas into

chapters or topics. If you're writing a novel, you might organize your ideas into acts or scenes.

3. Just like the human body has a structure to hold itself together, so needs a book. It's time to create a skeleton outline. Using your organized ideas, create a skeletal structured outline of your book. This should include the major sections, acts, or chapters of your story. Then write a summary of what will be covered in each.

4. Just like the human body has its skeletal structure, and all the parts or organs which are covered with flesh and skin, once you have all the info, your skeleton outline will fill out. Each chapter is the bone structure, and the ideas developed in your paragraphs are the flesh. So, start fleshing out each section. Add more details and structure to each section and break each section down into sub-sections if necessary. This will help you to create a more detailed and cohesive outline.

5. As you now have a more detailed outline, refine, and revise it as necessary. It is a living creation and will grow. During this process you can make sure it flows well, and that each section or chapter not only builds upon the previous one, but ultimately each chapter leads the reader forward into the next. You might find that you need to move things around or add/remove sections to make it work better as your creation comes to life.

6. Once you're happy with your outline you can begin to finalize it. This process will serve as your roadmap for writing your book, so make sure it's comprehensive and well-organized. Just as you use the map APP on your phone today to guide you to where you are driving you need a roadmap for writing your book.

Keep in mind, the key to creating a good outline is to be organized and focused. Take the time to brainstorm and organize your ideas, and don't be afraid to revise and refine your outline as needed. With a solid outline in place, you'll have a clear roadmap for writing your book. Make note that just because you have created this roadmap for writing your book, just as in life, as you move forward you might find a new path that you would rather take than where the APP is telling you to drive.

Perhaps you might all of a sudden kill off your protagonist. Now, you need to find your new direction. If you do choose to step outside of your created roadmap as you are writing your book and you decide to take a new path into a new direction it is best to stop and recreate your new path. It is okay that you might change your mind and go in a new direction, but you must then recreate a new set of coordinates for your APP to now guide you on your new path. So, recreate your new outline as you set out on your new path to complete your book.

So, let's brainstorm!

What is your plot?

_____

_____

_____

_____

_____

How about your general concept, themes, characters, and
scenes_____

_____

_____

_____

_____

CREATING YOUR CHARACTERS

In addition to the protagonist/antagonist, there are several other types of characters that can be found in a book. You will notice in such epic books- as Lord of The Rings, Harry Potter, and Game of Thrones, you will find a myriad of character types and styles. Not all books will have all of these types, however, upon reflection you will recognize who in your own life plays the part of each one of the following types.

1. Sidekick/Ally: This character often supports the protagonist and helps them achieve their goals. They may provide assistance, guidance, or moral support throughout the story.

2. Mentor/Guide: The mentor is a wise and experienced character who guides the protagonist, offering advice,

teaching skills, and providing important insights. They often play a pivotal role in the protagonist's journey.

3. Love Interest: This character forms a romantic or emotional connection with the protagonist and plays a significant role in their personal development. The love interest can add depth and complexity to the story, often serving as a motivation or conflict for the protagonist.

4. Foil: A foil character is designed to contrast with the protagonist, highlighting their strengths, weaknesses, or different perspectives. The foil may be an ally or an antagonist, but their purpose is to create tension and emphasize certain qualities in the protagonist.

5. Supporting Characters: These characters fill out the story's world and interact with the main characters. They may be friends, family members, colleagues, or acquaintances who contribute to the plot or provide additional perspectives. While they may not have as much screen time as the protagonist and antagonist, they play important roles in the overall narrative.

6. Comic Relief: A character who provides humor and light-hearted moments in the story. They often have a knack for funny or eccentric behavior, providing relief from tension or drama.

7. Villain's Henchmen: These characters serve as the minions or subordinates of the antagonist. They may carry out the antagonist's orders, provide support, or act as obstacles for the protagonist.

8. Anti-hero: An anti-hero is a complex character who possesses both heroic and flawed qualities. They may have selfish motivations, engage in morally ambiguous actions, or struggle with internal conflicts. Despite their shortcomings, they may ultimately do the right thing or play a significant role in the story.

9. Cameo/Minor Characters: These characters appear briefly or have minimal impact on the overall plot but contribute to the world-building or add flavor to the story. They may appear in a single scene or have a few lines of dialogue.

These are just a few examples of the many types of characters that can be found in a book. The specific combination and dynamics of characters will depend on the story and the author's creative choices.

What characters do you envision? Make sure to make them believable — even if they are only supporting characters.

Using the characters from the previous worksheet, let's build your characters.

Who is your main character, what are their traits, strengths/weaknesses (make them into a human you would like), what is their back story?

Who is your Sidekick/Ally?

_____

_____

_____

_____

_____

Mentor/Guide?

_____

_____

_____

_____

_____

Love interest?

___

Supporting characters?

___

Foil/Comic relief?

___

Villain's Henchman?

_____
_____
_____
_____
_____
_____
_____

Antihero?

_____
_____
_____
_____
_____

Cameo/minor characters?

_____
_____

CREATING YOUR SCENES AND SETTINGS

Another thing to understand is the strength of your scene or setting creations. World creation for fantasy writing is what helps make or break an epic. When looking at epic films such as the Star Wars saga, Avatar, or Lord of the Rings as an example you can begin to understand the nuance and power of creating worlds and settings. When outlining the settings for chapters in your book, it's essential to create a vivid and immersive world that enhances your story. I look at the scenes, settings, and world creation as another character in the story itself.

1. Consider the role the setting plays in each chapter. Does it provide a backdrop for a significant event, create a specific mood or atmosphere, or reveal something

about the characters? Understanding the purpose will help you choose appropriate settings.

_____

_____

_____

_____

_____

2. Imagine the physical aspects of the setting in detail. Visualize the geography, architecture, climate, and other relevant elements. This will help you describe the setting accurately and make it come alive for your readers.

Geography_____

_____

_____

_____

_____

Architecture

_____

_____

_____

_____

_____

Climate:

_____
_____
_____
_____
_____

3. Conduct research to gather information and inspiration for your setting. Read books, watch movies, or explore real-world locations that are similar to what you have in mind. Collect visual references, maps, or historical details that can enrich your descriptions. What research do you have? Visual References? Maps? Historical details? Make sure to also have all citations.

Visual References:

_____
_____
_____
_____
_____

Maps:

___

___

___

___

Historical References:

___

___

___

___

Citations:

___

___

___

___

___

4. Focus on sensory details to bring the setting to life. Describe the sights, sounds, smells, textures, and tastes associated with the location. Engaging multiple senses will make the setting more vivid and immersive.
What sensory details can you use?

_____

_____

_____

_____

_____

5. If your story is set in a specific time period, ensure that the setting reflects the characteristics of that era. Research the historical, cultural, and societal elements that influence the location, language, styles of clothing, and even foods, and incorporate them into your descriptions. Make sure that the wording of dialogues is consistent with the time period.
Notate a few to help you to build your story line:

_____

_____

_____

_____

_____

_____

6. The setting should align with the mood and tone you want to convey in each chapter. For example, a dark and gloomy forest might be suitable for a suspenseful or mysterious scene, while a vibrant and bustling cityscape might be ideal for an energetic or romantic moment. List some settings you might use.

_____

_____

_____

_____

_____

chapter. Is it tranquil, foreboding, celebratory, or chaotic? Consider the lighting, weather conditions, and overall ambiance that contribute to the desired atmosphere.

_____

_____

_____

_____

_____

8. Think about how the characters interact with the setting. Does it pose challenges, offer opportunities, or evoke certain emotions? The interaction between characters and their environment can deepen the reader's understanding of both.

_____
_____
_____
_____
_____

9. Ensure that the settings for each chapter offer variety and progression throughout the story. Varying the locations can prevent monotony and provide opportunities for new experiences and plot developments.

_____
_____
_____
_____
_____

10. Create a brief outline or summary of each setting for your chapters. Include the main features, notable landmarks, and any specific elements that are crucial to

the plot or character development. This outline will serve as a reference while writing and help you maintain consistency_____

_____ _____

_____

_____

_____

Remember that settings are not just backdrops but integral parts of your storytelling. By carefully outlining and describing your settings, you can transport readers into the world of your book and enhance their reading experience.

_____

_____

_____

_____

_____

More Notes

_____

_____

FOLLOWING YOUR OUTLINE TO WRITE YOUR BOOK

Now, you can see how creating an outline for your book can help you to organize your ideas, plan your chapters, and ensure that your writing flows smoothly. Next begins the task of writing your book. One of the first things you must do as a writer is to find your writing style. Developing your own personal writing style is an ongoing process that involves honing your skills, finding your unique voice, and continuously refining your craft. This is done by writing, reading, and thinking. It is about taking the time to sit with your thoughts and watch them. It is about taking the time to read other people's process and seeing if it rings true for you. Here are some tips to help you develop your writing style.

1. Read books, articles, and other forms of writing across various genres and styles. Expose yourself to different writing voices and techniques. Analyze and appreciate the writing styles of authors you admire and take note of what resonates with you. You might like to read Shakespeare; however, you know that is not how you want to write. What you put into your brain helps dictate what comes out.

What is your genre?_____

Style?_____

What voice will you be using?_____

What authors resonate with you?_____

What do you like most about their writing?_____

2. One thing is key – if you want to be a writer you need to write. It doesn't matter what you write but write! Eventually, your voice will begin to show itself. The more you write, the more you will develop and refine your own style. Treat your writing with respect. Set aside dedicated time for writing and make it a habit.

Write in different genres and experiment with different styles to find what suits you best.

What style do you like best?

_____

What genre are you most comfortable with?_____

3. You will eventually find your voice. Or it will find you. Your writing style should reflect your unique perspective and personality. Don't be afraid to let your personality shine through your writing. You are a unique individual, so know that your point of view is unique to the world. Write authentically and express your thoughts and emotions in a way that feels true to you.

4. Don't be afraid to experiment with different techniques. Try different writing techniques and approaches to timing and the rhythms of words. Don't be afraid to play with sentence structures, use of metaphors, descriptive language, pacing, and dialogue. Explore different narrative perspectives and points of view. You might begin something using a first-person narrative and

realize that the story will resonate better if it is in third person. You can also interject in a different voice to use for something such as a dream sequence. This experimentation will help you discover what resonates with you and what makes your writing distinct.

5. Remember to edit and revise. Take the time to review and revise your work. Pay attention to your word choices, sentence structure, and overall flow. Refine your writing to ensure it aligns with your intended style and tone. Each writer is different. Bukowski's style is different from Hemingway and John Steinbeck is different from Mark Twain. Some writers don't edit and revise until they complete what they feel is their entire manuscript. Some writers might edit and revise after completing each chapter. You will find what works for you as you move forward.

6. Asking for feedback can be hard. But seek feedback. When you do you must do so with the auspice that you are ready to hear it no matter what it is. It is to be constructive. So, choose who you want to show it to. Share your writing with trusted friends, fellow writers, or writing groups and seek their feedback. Their

perspectives can help you identify strengths and areas for improvement in your writing style. Take the feedback into consideration. Let go of your ego and listen to how they might describe your style. You might find that you lose your reader, or things aren't flowing the way you intended. Keep an open mind so you can hear the feedback. It can be hard to disassociate yourself with your story during this process, but if you do it can be very helpful. Do you have alpha/beta readers set up yo give you meaningful input?

7. Learn to embrace your influences. While developing your own style, it's natural to be influenced by the writers you admire. Embrace those influences but strive to find your own unique voice within them. If you find you are more naturally influenced by a more poetic style rather than a fast-paced thriller style, embrace your own style. Don't fight it. It is showing itself to you so you can best deliver your story. Remember that developing your writing style is a journey that takes time and practice. Be patient, keep writing, and allow yourself the freedom to evolve and grow as a writer.

NOTES

EDITING YOUR BOOK

The next step to creating a book is to edit your book. There are millions of books created each year and many are now self-published. What many writers fail to understand is the importance of editing your manuscript. Getting your manuscript edited by a professional editor is not always in a writer's budget, but you must keep in mind it is one of the most important processes of creating a successful book. Here are some steps you can take prior to giving your book to a professional. But it is advised that before you finally publish you find a professional editor that has worked with the style of book you are creating and understands the nuances of editing a book of that genre.

1. Take a break from writing before you begin to edit. After you've finished writing your book, take a break from it for a little while. This will help you come back to it with fresh eyes and allow you to see it more objectively. For some authors that break might mean a day and for others it might mean longer. But separate yourself from your story enough to clear your internal cache.

2. Now, find a quiet place different from where you sit to write and simply read through your book. Read through your book from beginning to end, making note of any errors or areas that need improvement as you go. You can do this on paper or on your computer, depending on your preference. You can use pens, pencils, colored pencils, sticky notes, or whatever means works best for you.

3. Soon you will have identified your areas for improvement. As you read through your book and identify areas that need improvement you might also review the cohesiveness of your style. This process helps you define your writing. The areas of improvement might include grammar or spelling errors, inconsistencies in the plot or characters, or sections that feel unclear or confusing.

4. It is good to learn to prioritize changes. Once you've identified areas for improvement, prioritize.

5. Once you have found all your areas that need changes it is time to revise and rewrite. As you make changes, revise, and rewrite your book by following your editing notes. This might also involve reordering chapters, rewriting sections, or even adding or removing entire scenes. There is nothing to be afraid of here. This is your chance to shine at development of your creation. You are in the driver's seat of your creation. Don't be afraid if you find that chapter 3 needs to become chapter 13. If it makes your book flow better than your original outline, now is the time to make that change.

6. Once again it's time to get feedback. Once you've made your revisions, get feedback from others. You can do this per chapter or as a whole. This could be from beta readers, a writing group, or an editor. Use their feedback to further refine and improve your book. It is good for a writer to have a cadre of people that understand the writing process and know what part of the process you are in in order to give you appropriate feedback. So, join groups, talk to editors, talk to beta readers to know who is best for you to work with on your project.

7. Most writers use some kind of editing software during their writing process for grammar and spelling. After you've made all the necessary revisions, edit your book for grammar and spelling errors. You can do this yourself using some software or hire a professional editor. If you want to make the best book possible, I suggest you do both. The more eyes finding the errors the better. But you also must keep in mind that there is no such thing as perfection. Constantly trying to be perfect can stagnate the process. Too much analysis can create paralysis.

8. Now, once you're happy with your edits, you have reached the point of finalizing your book. This will involve formatting it for publication, creating a cover design, or submitting it to a publisher or literary agent. There is a myriad of processes to create a successful book. Writing and editing are simply part of that process. To get your book to print you will need to format it for either soft cover, hard cover, e-book, or even record it for audiobook. Overall, the key to editing your book is to be thorough and diligent. Take the time to read through your book carefully, and don't be afraid to make significant changes if needed. With careful editing, you can turn your book into a polished and professional piece of work.

NOTES:

DESIGNING YOUR COVER

Designing a book cover for hard copy, soft copy, and e-book can involve different steps and considerations. Each part of the book creating process can be as creative as you make it. Make sure you are aware of the styles that work best for your book format.

1. Before you start designing your cover, determine the format of your book. A hard copy will have different dimensions than a soft copy or e-book. You might find that you will need to make different cover art styles for your book for each format. What are your ideas?

_____
_____

_____

_____

_____

_____

2. Look at book covers in your genre to get an idea of design trends and what has worked well for other authors. Brainstorm ideas for your own cover that reflect the tone, theme, and genre of your book. You may not want to be just like everyone else, but you don't want to be so different that it doesn't catch the eye of the buyer. What kinds of book covers do you find attractive? What elements would you like to see incorporated into the style, etc.

_____

_____

_____

_____

_____

3. Decide on the main design elements you want to include in your cover, such as typography, images, and color scheme.

4. If you don't have design experience or want a professional-looking cover, consider hiring a designer. You can find designers online through freelancing websites or by asking for recommendations from other authors. Remember you can't judge a book by its cover, but in the literary world that's exactly what happens. The cover art can make or break a book. research and list possibilities.

5. If you are working with a designer, provide them with a brief that includes information about your book, genre, and design preferences. Give feedback on initial concepts and work with the designer to refine the cover design. Maybe let them know of other books that you

like that are similar to what you are thinking of for yours. What will your brief/query to the cover designer say?-

_____
_____
_____
_____
_____

6. Depending on the format of your book, you may need to adjust the design of your cover. For example, an e-book cover may need to be optimized for digital display and have simpler design elements than a hard copy cover. Your hardcover may allow you to have copy and information on the inner covers, whereas your softcover will need to be laid out in a different way. What would you like the copy to say?

_____
_____
_____
_____
_____

7. Once you're happy with your cover design, finalize it by saving it in the correct file format for each format (e.g., JPEG for online publication, PDF for print). Overall, designing a cover for your book can take time and effort, but it's an important aspect of marketing your book and attracting readers. By following these steps and working with a designer if needed, you can create a professional and eye-catching cover for your book. There are several ways to find an artist to create artwork for your book and cover. List at least three options for your cover design.

_____

_____

_____

_____

_____

8. Online marketplaces such as Fiverr, Upwork, Reedsy and Freelancer can connect you with freelance artists who can create artwork for your book and cover. These platforms allow you to browse portfolios and reviews, and to communicate with artists to find the right fit for your project. You might also find through a shout out on your social media that you have someone in your circle of "friends" that could help you complete this task.

Research these sites and list what you like, etc.

_____
_____
_____
_____
_____

9. As I say, you can use social media platforms such as Twitter, Instagram, and LinkedIn to search for and connect with artists who specialize in book cover design and illustration. You can search for relevant hashtags and follow industry professionals to discover artists who may be a good fit for your project. What hashtags have brought you to cover designers or even artists that could create art used to illustrate?

_____
_____
_____
_____

10. You might also join different creative communities such as DeviantArt, Behance, and Dribbble to discover artists and designers who can create artwork for your book and cover. These platforms allow you to browse

portfolios and connect with artists who share your interests and aesthetics. research and give insights. What have you found that has caught your interest?

_____

_____

_____

_____

_____

11. Another way to find cover designers is to ask fellow authors, publishers, and industry professionals for referrals to artists who specialize in book cover design and illustration. Referrals can help you find trusted and experienced artists who have a proven track record of creating successful book covers and illustrations. Also, by doing this you will connect with others in your field and that same call could turn into a podcast interview later on. You never know how things can play out! Who/Where can you get referrals?

_____

_____

_____

_____

_____

Just make sure that when you are selecting an artist, you review their portfolio and past work to ensure their style aligns with your vision for your book and cover. Also, communicate your expectations clearly, including timelines, budget, and revisions, to ensure a successful collaboration. Also make sure artwork is original, and/or that all licensing is completed.

FORMATTING YOUR BOOK

Formatting a book for print can be a complex process. You want to create a book that is right for the genre that you are writing in. Whether you are creating a soft cover mystery novel, or a hard cover tabletop book, here are some basic steps you can follow to prepare your book for print. Depending on what firm you are using for your printing they might have their own rules to adhere to for your book production. You need to inquire as to the intricacies of their production needs as they pertain to your book and its desired needs. The paper stock for your mystery novel will be different than that of your tabletop book filled with artwork within the manuscript. These decisions will help dictate what might better serve your specific book style. This is a very specialized part of the process and can create many headaches and delays. It is best to use a professional for this process.

1. You must figure out your book's size. The first step in formatting your book is to choose a trim size. This refers to the size of your book and can vary depending on the type of book you're publishing. As an example, common trim sizes for novels and non-fiction books are 5.5 x 8.5 inches or 6 x 9 inches.

What size do you want?_____

Is the trim you've decided upon large enough for your page count?_____

2. Once you've chosen a trim size, it's time to set up your margins and gutters. Margins should be at least 0.5 inches on all sides and can be adjusted as needed depending on the size of your book, while gutters should be set at mirroring. What are your margins and gutters set at? Does the genre you are writing in have a standard?

_____
_____
_____
_____
_____

3. Getting the right font to use for your book can be a creative process in itself. Choose fonts for your book's body text and headings. For body text, a serif font such as Times New Roman or Garamond is often used. For headings, you can choose a sans-serif font such as Arial or Helvetica, or you can use the same font as your text. Make note you can use this process to be creative with your book, but you must also keep in mind what fonts can be embedded as required for the production cycle of the platform or company you have chosen for your printing. The embedded fonts command can be chosen under File and once chosen, remains the standard for all files you share. On your computer in your Word program go to File/option/advanced/preserve fidelity/embed linguistic material (fonts).What font do you wish to use? You may also use different fonts for your title page. If so, what fonts are you thinking of?

_____
_____
_____
_____
_____
_____

4. Set up page numbers for the header or footer of your document. Page numbers are normally centered at the bottom of the page. However, some people choose to have the page numbers in the upper or lower right-side corners. Again, this is a creative and style decision for your project and can be found under the reference tab and applied to your Word document. Make sure to use section breaks correctly for your chapters, and to format your page numbers correctly so that they are sequential and start on the first page of text, and not on title, copyright, or table of contents pages.

5. Next you need to format each chapter title with a clear heading, adjusting font, etc to chapter titles. These must be formatted to allow for the next step of adding the Table of Contents. Also, make sure these chapters start on a new page. Does the platform or publisher require you to start these new chapter pages on the odd page? Do they require the book to end on an even page number? What are the specifications of the platform/publisher which you will use? Knowing these criteria while formatting saves much time and frustration. This research saves you great time as it is how you complete the next step – the Table of Contents. What is your publisher's/printer's requirements on page formatting?

_____

_____

_____

_____

_____

6. You should also include a table of contents (TOC) at the beginning section of the book. You will find the autoformatted one in the references ribbon of your word processer. The TOC comes after the copyright page. The TOC will auto-populate from the headings, or chapter titles, you have created when you choose to update table.

7. Another requirement will be your copyright page. This page has all of the publisher's information, copyright date, ISBN numbers, author information, website, cover artist, publisher's information, and website, and more. Research these and list what you have already.

_____

_____

_____

_____

_____

8. If your book includes images, make sure they are high resolution and properly sized. Talk to your printer as they will have specific needs to this. They might expect your images to be saved in profile of CMYK, or they might also prefer PDFs for all of their files. You can also add captions or labels as needed. Adding the copyright information of the artist or photographer to the metadata may be needed. What color profile does your printer require? What file formats are required? What resolution is required?

_____

_____

_____

_____

_____

9. Once you've completed the formatting for your book, double-check everything to ensure it is consistent and looks professional. What size are your headings? Are they all consistent? Is line spacing consistent? How about your text?

_____

_____

_____

_____

10. Convert your book to a PDF format, which is a standard format for printing. Make sure to save your file with a clear and descriptive name. Sometimes when you send it to your printer you might uncover some formatting issues. Creating a clear and concise file naming process can help you as it may take numerous attempts to finalize your files for the printer.

11. Finally, submit your final PDF file to a printer or publishing service for printing. Make sure to choose a reputable printer with high-quality printing services. Overall, formatting a book for print can be a detailed process, but following these steps can help you create a professional and polished final product.

PUBLISHING YOUR BOOK

Getting your book published and available in all bookstores can be a challenging process. Many authors claim it is best to self-publish because you get to keep all of your profit. However, you may have already surmised that creating has many tasks that most people simply will not or cannot do successfully. That is why there are professionals that can help each step of the way. Sure, self-publishing means you get to keep 100% of everything, but if you create a book that sells only 50 copies you only get to keep 100% of 50 copies.

1. There are several different publishing options available, including traditional publishing, hybrid publishing, and self-publishing. Research each option to determine which one is the best fit for you and your

book. Remember that 90% of all self-published books sell only 100 copies. Working with a hybrid publisher means you don't have to look for the editors, alpha/beta readers, typesetters, formatters, artists, designers, printers, and others that help you create your book as they have these specialists at their ready for you. Although, this comes at a fee, it is key to remember that either way you will pay. Will you undertake all of the jobs it takes to self-publish, where you pay with your own time and energy and confusion and frustration to *finally control everything* and sell only 100 copies, or will you work with a firm that has all of the people and parts in place to help you do what you love to do more, which is to write? Let us help you. Let professionals take it from here. Chances are your book will be more successful in the long run.

2. Remember, before you can publish your book, you need to have a polished manuscript. This may involve multiple rounds of editing and revising. As we described previously, this can be a daunting process if you are not familiar with the process. Or, you can save yourself all the frustration and have your publisher take care of the process, using their knowledge of the publishing field to make your book the best it can be.

3. If you are working with a hybrid or small boutique publisher, chances are you can find this publishing partner on your own. If you are trying to break into the traditional route of publishing, you will need to find a literary agent. There are very few traditional publishers that accept unsolicited material. If you don't know anyone with the publishing firm, chances are they will not read your manuscript unless you have an agent. So, if you're interested in traditional publishing, you may want to consider finding a literary agent. Literary agents can help you get your book in front of publishers and negotiate contracts on your behalf. The agent fee will eat into your profit of your final contract; however, chances are if you reach this point your book will sell more than 100 copies. Who is your literary agent? Or what are the names of some?

_____
_____
_____
_____
_____

Are you going to self-publish or are you going to let others, who know the process, help you to get your manuscript published?

4. Once you have a polished manuscript and/or a literary agent, you can start submitting your book to publishers. Some publishers only accept submissions through agents, while others might accept unsolicited manuscripts. What publishers accept submissions without a literary agent?

_____

_____

_____

_____

_____

5. If you don't want to go through traditional publishing channels, you can consider self-publishing. Self-publishing involves taking on the responsibilities of editing, formatting, and marketing your book yourself. Not everyone has the capacity, patience, and tenacity to do all that is necessary to self-publish. So, attempting to do so if you are not someone with that capacity can be very detrimental to your book ever seeing the light of day.

6. There are several self-publishing platforms available, such as Amazon KDP, IngramSpark, Draft2Digital and more. Research each platform to determine which one is the best fit for your book and your publishing goals.

There are pluses and minuses with each and a stringent learning curve, but after doing your research you will find what can work best for you. What self-publishing platforms interest you, and what are their requirements?

_____
_____
_____
_____
_____
_____

7. Depending on the platform you choose, you will need to prepare your book for publication by formatting it, designing a cover, and uploading it to the platform, as we described previously. Each platform has different rules and regulations that need to be met. You will need to research what is best for you before you go through that process.

8. Once your book is finally published, you'll need to market it to potential readers. This may involve building a website, using social media, and running advertising campaigns. Again, this is a whole other learning curve

of technology and information that will be necessary to understand if you are to be self-publishing.

9. If you self-publish, in order to get your book into bookstores, you'll need to approach them directly. This may involve sending them copies of your book and promotional materials, or scheduling book signings and events. Self-publishing can be a very rewarding process if you can maneuver through the maze of tasks necessary. Overall, getting your book published and available in all bookstores can be a complex and challenging process. However, by taking these steps and being persistent in your efforts, you can increase your chances of success.

NOTES

_____
_____
_____
_____
_____

A QUERY LETTER TO FIND YOUR AGENT

If you are deciding to attempt to go the traditional publishing route you will need to construct a query letter. There are some hybrid publishing houses that may ask you for a query letter, as well. A query letter is your introduction to literary agents and is typically the first thing they see when considering your book for representation. Here is a guide to follow when writing a query letter for your book.

1. Start your query letter with a strong hook that grabs the agent's attention and makes them want to read more. This could be a brief summary of your book's plot or a statement about what makes your book unique.

2. In the second paragraph(section), provide a brief synopsis of your book. This should include the main characters, the central conflict, and the setting. Keep this section brief, typically no more than a few paragraphs.

3. In the third paragraph), highlight any relevant credentials you have that make you the ideal person to write this book. This could include any previous writing experience, relevant education, or personal experiences that inform your book.

4. In the final paragraph, thank the agent for their time and consideration, and include your contact information. You may also want to briefly mention any other relevant information, such as if you have other completed manuscripts or if your book has won any awards.

5. Keep your query letter to one page or less, and make sure that it is free from errors or typos. Remember to personalize your query letter for each agent you are submitting to and follow their submission guidelines carefully. A well-crafted query letter can help you to stand out from the many other submissions an agent receives and increase your chances of securing representation for your book.

NOTES

MARKETING YOUR BOOK

Marketing your book is an important part of the publishing process, and there are several strategies you can use to get the word out and increase sales. Today's technology gives you a wide variety of options available to market your book. Each one of these items is imperative to creating a successful book and each one has a distinct learning curve in order to accomplish.

1. It is imperative you create a website that can serve as a central hub for your book and help you establish a professional online presence. You can use your website to showcase your book, offer sample chapters or excerpts, and provide information about upcoming events. You will need to research companies that generate your own website, or whether you choose a

company who specializes in building websites for customers.

___

2. Social media platforms like Facebook, Twitter, Instagram, and LinkedIn can be powerful tools for promoting your book and connecting with potential readers. Consider creating dedicated accounts for your book and posting regularly to build engagement. You can hire a professional whose entire business model is focused on just this process and many of the other tasks associated with creating and publishing your book. Take the time to find the right team that will work best for you. That is one of the benefits of using a hybrid or traditional publisher. They already have a team and processes in place to help create your successful book. What platforms are you currently familiar with? What sites will you have pages on? How much time can you set aside to regularly interact with potential customers?

3. Paid advertising campaigns on social media, search engines, or book discovery platforms can help you reach a wider audience. Consider setting a budget and targeting your ads to readers who are likely to be interested in your book. How much are the advertising costs on Facebook, LinkedIn, or even Google?

4. Influencers, such as book bloggers, podcasters, and reviewers, can help you reach new readers and build buzz around your book. Research influencers in your genre and reach out to them to offer a review copy or ask for a feature.

_____
_____
_____
_____
_____

5. Attending events and book signings can help you connect with readers in person and build a local following. Consider scheduling events at local bookstores, libraries, or literary festivals. What authors' groups are in your area? Bookfairs?

_____
_____
_____
_____

6. Promotions and giveaways can help you generate buzz and incentivize readers to buy your book. Consider offering a limited-time discount or running a giveaway on social media. Research what works and how you could use.

_____

7. Email marketing can be an effective way to reach readers who have already shown interest in your book. Consider building an email list and sending regular newsletters with updates, promotions, and exclusive content. Overall, marketing your book requires a multi-faceted approach that includes both online and offline strategies. By being persistent and strategic in your efforts, you can increase your book's visibility and generate more sales. Just as with any product that is for sale in this world, it all comes down to marketing and getting your work out there to as many people as you can. What marketing will you use?

CREATING YOUR WEBSITE

Setting up a website for your book can be a great way to establish a professional online presence and promote your book to potential readers. This will be something that is forever online and giving your book the longevity, it needs to create long-term sales.

1. Take the time to figure out your domain name. Your domain name is the address people will use to access your website (e.g., www.booktitle.com). Choose a domain name that is memorable and easy to type. Choose a title that references or is familiar to you, the author or the name of your book, or both.-

_____
_____
_____

2. There are several website platforms available, such as WordPress, Wix, and Squarespace. Research each platform to determine which one is the best fit for your needs and budget.

_____
_____
_____
_____
–

3. Once you've selected a website platform, choose a template that is appropriate for your book and genre. Many platforms offer customizable templates that you can modify to suit your needs. List the template chosen.

_____
_____
_____
_____
_____

4. Customize your website so that it creates your brand by adding pages, uploading images, and writing content. Consider including a page about yourself, a page about your book, and a page with sample chapters or excerpts.

_____
_____
_____
_____
_

5. If you plan on selling your book directly through your website, you'll need to add e commerce functionality. Many website platforms offer built-in e commerce tools or integrations with popular e commerce platforms like Shopify or WooCommerce. Or you could format your site to include your own account with Stripe or Venmo. What e-commerce tools do you like? Will the tool work with your bank account?

_____
_____
_____
_____
_____

6. Optimizing your website for search engines (SEO) can help you rank higher in search results and attract more visitors. Consider researching relevant keywords

and including them in your website content and metadata.

_____
_____
_____
_____

Before launching your website, test it thoroughly to ensure that everything works as expected. Once you're satisfied, launch your website, and promote it to potential readers through social media, email marketing, and other channels. Overall, setting up a website for your book can be a valuable marketing tool that can help you reach a wider audience and establish a professional online presence. By following these steps and being persistent in your efforts, you can create a website that effectively promotes your book and attracts readers.

CREATING A PODCAST

Setting up a podcast requires several steps, but it can be a great way to reach new audiences and promote your book. The media industry has gone through some dramatic changes in recent years and podcasting has become a very popular means of gaining attention and followers throughout the world.

1. Choose a topic that is relevant to your book and that you are passionate about. Determine the format of your podcast, such as interviews, solo episodes, or a mix of both.

2. In order to record your podcast properly and professionally, you'll need a microphone, headphones, and audio editing software. There are many options

available, from basic USB microphones to more advanced setups.

3. Record your podcast episodes using your chosen equipment and software. Edit your episodes to remove any mistakes or unnecessary content.

4. Choose a podcast hosting platform, such as Substack, Libsyn, Buzzsprout, or Podbean, to host your podcast. There are more out there. Just research and see what best platform will work best for you. These platforms will store your audio files and distribute them to podcast directories like Apple Podcasts and Spotify.

5. Submit your podcast-to-podcast directories, such as Apple Podcasts, Spotify, and Google Podcasts.

6. Promote your podcast through your website, social media, and other channels. Encourage listeners to leave reviews and ratings to help increase your podcast's visibility.

7. Consistency is key when it comes to podcasting. Create a regular schedule for your podcast episodes and stick to it. Overall, setting up a podcast requires some initial investment in equipment and software, but can be a great way to reach new audiences and promote your book. By following these steps and being persistent in

your efforts, you can create a successful podcast that attracts listeners and helps grow your audience.

NOTES

CREATING A FOLLOWING

Getting followers to your website and podcast is a key part of promoting your book and generating sales. None of this happens overnight. Remember the book world is a slow pace. It can take some time to create a following so patience is a key factor in the marketing and promotional side of the business.

1. Make sure your website and podcast are optimized for search engines (SEO) so that they appear in search results when people are looking for information on topics related to your book. Use relevant keywords in your content, titles, and metadata. Again, you can hire a professional whose entire business model is focused on just this process.

2. Promote your website and podcast on social media platforms like Twitter, Facebook, and Instagram. Share links to your website and podcast episodes and engage with your followers by responding to comments and questions.

3. Consider guest blogging or guest podcasting on other websites and podcasts in your niche. This can help you reach new audiences and establish yourself as an authority in your field.

4. Provide valuable content on your website and podcast that resonates with your audience. This could be in the form of blog posts, articles, videos, or podcast episodes that provide useful information, tips, or insights.

5. Build an email list of subscribers who are interested in your book and content. Send regular newsletters and updates to keep them engaged and informed about your latest work.

6. Join forums and online communities related to your book's topic or genre and engage with members by answering questions, sharing insights, and promoting your website and podcast.

7. Offer giveaways and promotions on your website and social media platforms to encourage people to follow you and share your content with others. By implementing these strategies, you can attract more followers to your website and podcast, build a community of loyal fans, and ultimately generate more book sales.

NOTES

BUILD YOUR ONLINE PRESENCE

Getting featured on other podcasts is a great way to build your online presence and reach new audiences. This can be difficult but a powerful way to use other people's audience to grow your own.

1. Look for podcasts that cover topics related to your book and that have a similar target audience. Make a list of potential podcasts to target.

2. Follow the podcasts and the hosts on social media and engage with their content. Leave thoughtful comments and share their content with your own followers. This can help you build a relationship with the host and make it easier to pitch yourself as a guest.

3. Develop a pitch that highlights your expertise and explains why you would be a valuable guest on the podcast. Include details about your book and the topics you can speak on. Make sure your pitch is personalized to the specific podcast and host you are targeting.

4. Send your pitch to the podcast host via email or social media. Make sure to follow up if you don't hear back after a week or two.

5. If you are invited to be a guest on a podcast, be prepared and professional. Show up on time, engage with your moderator, and provide value to the listeners. Make sure to promote the episode on your own social media channels to help drive traffic to the podcast. By following these tips, you can increase your chances of getting featured on other podcasts and building your online presence. It's important to remember that building relationships and providing value to others is key to success in the podcasting world.

NOTES

MASS MEDIA PROMOTION

Getting your book promoted in magazines, newspapers, television, and podcasts can help you reach a wider audience and generate more book sales. This can be very difficult to get yourself in, but if you can it can be effective. You can hire a professional whose entire business model is focused on just this process.

1. Identify media outlets that cover topics related to your book and that have a similar target audience. Make a list of potential outlets to target. Remember, you can hire a professional whose entire business model is focused on just this process.

2. Create a media kit that includes information about your book, your author bio, high-resolution images of your book cover and author photo, and any other relevant information. This will help media outlets quickly and easily access information about your book.

3. Develop a press release that highlights the key aspects of your book and why it's newsworthy. Make sure to customize the press release for each media outlet you are targeting.

4. Contact journalists and producers at the media outlets you are targeting via email or social media. Make sure to personalize your message and explain why your book is a good fit for their audience.

5. Offer to provide a free review copy of your book to journalists and producers who are interested in covering your book.

6. If you are contacted by a journalist or producer, be available for interviews and provide thoughtful and engaging answers.

7. Share any coverage of your book on your own social media channels and website to help promote it to your own audience. By following these steps, you can increase your chances of getting your book promoted in

magazines, newspapers, television, and podcasts, and ultimately reach a wider audience. It's important to remember that building relationships with journalists and producers and providing value to their audiences is key to success in the media world.

NOTES

THE BUSINESS OF WRITING

Remember that you are a writer in the publishing business. Being a writer is in itself a process. This means that you might find it beneficial to set yourself up as a business in the beginning to better control your position if your book takes off. Setting up a corporation for your writing business can help protect your personal assets and provide tax advantages.

1. Choose a unique name for your corporation that isn't already taken by another business.

2. There are different types of corporations, including LLC and S corporations. Depending on your level of attained success there is also a C corporation. Consider consulting with an attorney or accountant to determine

the best type of corporation for your specific business needs.

3. File articles of incorporation with the Secretary of State's office in the state where you plan to incorporate. This document will include information about the corporation's name, purpose, location, and other details.

4. Depending on your state and local laws, you may need to obtain permits and licenses to operate your business.

5. Create bylaws that outline how the corporation will be run, including details about shareholders, board of directors, meetings, and other governance matters.

6. Hold an initial meeting with the board of directors to adopt the bylaws, elect officers, and manage other organizational matters.

7. Apply for an Employer Identification Number (EIN) from the IRS. This is a unique number that will be used to identify your corporation for tax purposes.

8. Open a separate bank account for your corporation to keep your business finances separate from your personal finances.

9. Register for any necessary state and local taxes, such as sales tax or income tax. These are the general steps for setting up a corporation for your writing business. However, it's important to consult with an attorney and accountant to ensure you are following all the necessary legal and financial requirements for your specific situation.

NOTES

BECOMING A THOUGHT LEADER AND BRAND

Getting booked as an expert in podcasts and interviews can easily lead to speaking engagements that can help you establish yourself as a thought leader with your writing business. Remember you wrote a book. You are considered an expert in many eyes of the world. That is just how it works.

1. Determine your areas of expertise and focus on speaking engagements that align with your expertise. What are these engagements?

2. Create a speaker profile that highlights your experience, areas of expertise, and previous speaking

engagements. Include testimonials from previous event organizers or attendees if possible.

3. Research events that align with your expertise and target audience and reach out to event organizers with your speaker profile and pitch. You can find events by searching online directories or using social media to follow relevant organizations and event pages. Find out your contacts for your local libraries, community colleges or universities, and even coffee houses that may host writing events.

4. Consider joining a speaker bureau, which can help connect you with speaking opportunities and provide additional exposure to event organizers.

5. Attend networking events in your industry or topic area to meet potential event organizers and make connections.

6. Practice your speaking skills and create engaging presentations to impress event organizers and audiences.

7. Consider offering lower fees for your first speaking engagements to build your reputation and gain exposure. Once you establish yourself as a successful speaker, you can increase your fees. By following these steps, you can increase your chances of getting booked as an expert

in speaking engagements and promoting your writing business. Remember to always be professional and persistent, and continually seek out new speaking opportunities to expand your reach. There are several ways to find speaking gigs around the United States.

8. Online directories such as SpeakerMatch, National Speakers Association, and Women's Speaker Association are great resources to find speaking gigs. You can search by location, topic, and event type.

9. Follow event calendars on websites such as Eventbrite, Meetup, and Facebook to stay up to date on events happening in your area. You can also filter events by location and topic.

10. Join industry organizations related to your area of expertise. These organizations often host events and conferences, providing opportunities to speak and network with others in your field.

11. Reach out to event organizers directly and pitch your expertise as a speaker. You can find contact information on event websites or by searching online for event organizers in your area.

12. Network with other speakers in your field and ask them for recommendations on events and organizations to contact.

13. Use social media to connect with event organizers, industry organizations, and other speakers. LinkedIn, Twitter, and Facebook are great platforms to connect with others in your industry. Using these strategies, you can find speaking gigs around the United States and expand your reach as a speaker. Remember to be professional, persistent, and always look for new opportunities to grow your speaking career.

To differentiate yourself from other writers and authors and sell more books and get more speaking engagements, it's important to identify and highlight what makes you unique. Here are some strategies to help you stand out.

1. Develop a unique writing style and voice that sets you apart from other authors in your genre. This can help you create a unique brand that readers and event organizers will remember.

2. Identify a niche within your genre and become an expert in that area. This can help you stand out as a thought leader and attract a dedicated audience.

3. Develop a strong online presence through your website, social media, and other online platforms. This can help you build your brand, connect with readers, and event organizers, and promote your books and speaking engagements.

4. Offer something new and valuable to readers and event organizers, such as unique perspectives, innovative ideas, or practical advice. This can help you stand out and attract attention.

5. Develop a strong personal brand that aligns with your writing and speaking topics. This can help you establish yourself as a recognizable and credible expert in your field.

7. Highlight your unique background and experiences in your writing and speaking engagements. This can help you create a unique brand and attract audiences who are interested in your story. By leveraging your unique strengths and developing a strong personal brand, you can differentiate yourself from other writers and authors and increase your chances of selling more books and getting more speaking engagements. Remember to

always be authentic and true to yourself, and to continually seek out new opportunities to grow your brand and connect with readers and event organizers.

NOTES

TRADEMARK YOUR BRAND

If you are an entrepreneur or executive type businessperson releasing a book in order to help you become a thought leader in your field, you will want to trademark yourself as a writer, your book, and your catch phrases you might design that come out through your book. You can file for a trademark with the United States Patent and Trademark Office (USPTO). Follow these steps:

1. Choose a unique name, catch phrases, or logo that you want to trademark. This name, phrase or logo should be distinctive and not likely to be confused with other writers or brands.

2. You need to conduct a trademark search on the USPTO website to ensure that your chosen name or logo is not already in use or registered by another writer or brand.

3. File a trademark application with the USPTO. This application should include your name, phrase or logo, a description of your writing services, and the class of goods and services that your trademark applies to.

4. Wait for the USPTO to review your application. This process can take several months, during which time the USPTO will determine whether your trademark is eligible for registration. You've seen the phrase "patent pending"? It's like that.

5. If your trademark application is approved, you will receive a trademark registration from the USPTO. This registration gives you exclusive rights to use your name or logo in connection with your writing services. It's important to note that the trademark process can be complex and time-consuming, so it may be helpful to consult with a trademark attorney to ensure that your application is filed correctly and that your trademark is protected.

NOTES

PROS AND CONS OF SELF, HYBRID AND TRADITIONAL PUBLISHING

There are some writers who are adamant and have it in them to take the time and learn all of these tasks. There are some people who know the value of time and money and want to simply move forward with spending their money with a hybrid house and getting their book done professionally without all of the headaches. They understand that they will make some money with their book, however, not lose all of their royalties by using a hybrid publisher. With a traditional publishing house, the industry has gotten pretty tight and there are very few first-time writers that will find a traditional publishing deal, that is unless you are a Prince named Harry, or perhaps you are the ex-First Lady of the United States named Michelle. With that said each publishing method has its own set of advantages and disadvantages. Here are some general pluses and minuses to consider for each publishing method.

Self-publishing:

Pluses:

- Complete creative control over the book
- Faster turnaround time for publishing
- Higher royalty rates than traditional publishing
- Ability to choose pricing and marketing strategies.
- More flexibility in book design and formatting
- No need to go through the agent or publisher submission process.

Minuses:

- More work and responsibility on the author to handle editing, cover design, formatting, distribution, and marketing.
- Higher upfront costs for editing, cover design, and other services
- No guaranteed distribution or bookstore placement
- Limited resources and connections for marketing and promotion

Hybrid publishing:

Pluses:

- More support and resources than self-publishing, including editing, cover design, formatting, and marketing.
- Some distribution and bookstore placement opportunities
- Some traditional publishing resources, such as editing and cover design, while retaining some creative control

Minuses:

- More expensive than self-publishing
- May not provide the same level of support and resources as traditional publishing.
- May not be recognized as a legitimate publishing credit by some in the industry.

Traditional publishing:

Pluses:

- Access to experienced editors, cover designers, and other professionals
- Established distribution and bookstore placement channels.
- More credibility and recognition in the publishing industry
- Advance payment and royalties

Minuses:

- Lower royalty rates than self-publishing or hybrid publishing
- Longer turnaround time for publishing
- Limited creative control and input from the author
- Competitive and challenging submission process, often requiring an agent.
- Less flexibility in pricing and marketing strategies

Ultimately, the best publishing method for an author will depend on their goals, resources, and preferences. Some authors may prefer the complete control and higher royalties of self-publishing, while others may prioritize the resources and credibility of traditional publishing. Hybrid publishing can provide a middle ground, but it is important to research and carefully evaluate potential publishers to ensure they are reputable and will provide the necessary support and resources.

NOTES

JOIN THE OLIVE PUBLISHING FAMILY

If you publish with us at Olive Publishing, LLC, what you get from us is the satisfaction of knowing your project is in the hands of a professional staff. We are a hybrid publishing firm with the care and detail of the traditional publishers. We help our writers through the entire writing process if necessary, beginning from their idea and a blank page on through helping set them up with all of the professional bells and whistles that will help make a book a success. We are in it for the long haul and understand all the levels of knowledge it takes to bring your creation to life!

Here is a simplified list of what you can get through Olive Publishing, LLC. We can create a program with each writer that is designed just for them and their professional needs and budget. We have traditional publishing deals for those with a book all ready and it simply knocks our socks off and we have hybrid publishing deals designed for all the various types of writers at all levels of their game. We have a publishing deal that will work for you no matter what your budget. Here is a list of many of the options that we can provide to make your book a success.

- Dedicated in house agent
- Ghost Writing
- Developmental Editing
- Copy Editing
- Line Editing
- Proofreading
- Formatting
- Book layout
- Cover design
- Type design
- Typesetting
- Managed printing and distribution (over 40K retailers worldwide incl. Amazon, B&N, and more)
- 4 ISBNs
- 4 Bar Codes

- 4 QR Codes
- Author Corp. (set up - state fees may apply)
- Author website (including podcast platform and site monetization)
- Book Website
- Email list merge and management
- Book promotional video
- Intellectual property to author
- Author copies (25 hard cover)
- 6 social media campaign
- Media campaign (FB, TW, IG, BookTok)
- Press Release (over 1000 digital/print global outlets)
- 4 Podcast interviews (over 12mo)
- Author book signing opportunities
- TEDx Talk global opportunities
- Kirkus Review
- Major media publication coverage (available)
- Book Funnel Marketing Campaign
- Audio book production

Click below to set an appointment to discuss your publishing needs!

https://strategy.olivepublishingllc.com/booking-page

Make sure to leave a review of our book online!

Find us at:

https://olivepublishingllc.com/

www.ingramcontent.com/pod-product-compliance
Lightning Source LLC
Chambersburg PA
CBHW070954080526
44587CB00015B/2307